THE MAYANS CALENDARS AND ADVANCED WRITING SYSTEM

HISTORY BOOKS AGE 9-12

Children's History Books

Speedy Publishing LLC

40 E. Main St. #1156

Newark, DE 19711

www.speedypublishing.com

Copyright 2017

The Mayans developed a remarkable empire in what is now Mexico and Central America. It lasted for over two thousand years. Let's learn about two of their remarkable developments: their calendars and their writing system.

Chichen Itza

THE MAYAN CULTURE

The Mayans developed their unique culture as early as 500 BCE. They started building their great cities and dominating the other tribes and cultures nearby. The Mayan Empire was still going strong two thousand years later, when Europeans arrived in search of gold and new territory.

The Mayans were defeated by the Europeans by 1697, but at least one million Mayan people still live and retain some of their culture in southern Mexico and in Guatemala, Honduras, and El Salvador.

MAYANS IN SOLOLA

The Mayans were students of the stars, of
the turning of the year and of the seasons.
They built their cities to serve in part as solar

MAYAN NOBLES

observatories, and they developed complicated calendars and ways of writing down histories of great leaders and important events.

THE MAYAN CALENDAR

THE MAYAN CALENDARS

We have one calendar that covers the year of 365 days, plus an extra day every four years. The Mayans had a calendar like that, but they also had a second calendar to track the cycle of great festivals, celebrations of the gods, and other important events.

On top of that, the Mayans combined the two calendars to create yet two more calendars, the "Calendar Round" and the "Long Count". The "Long Count" calendar tracks almost two million days before it starts again!

29
30

MAYAN SOLAR CALENDAR

THE SOLAR CALENDAR

The Mayans' 365-day calendar was called the "jaab". The jaab had 18 months of twenty days each, making 360 days. The last five days of the year were considered unlucky days and were grouped in their own little "month".

The Mayan solar calendar had 365 days, but the actual orbit of the Earth around the sun takes 365.25 days. Our calendar has an extra day about every four years (with certain exceptions) to keep the calendar correctly aligned—so summer happens when the days are warm in the Northern Hemisphere, and winter when the days are cold. Because the Mayan calendar didn't have a concept of leap-years, the calendar slowly gets out of coordination with the seasons.

MAYAN CALENDAR

When the Mayan calendar is painted or drawn, the days are in a large circle. Outside of each month, there is an image of an attitude, force, god, or character associated with that month. This works sort of like astrology, where there are thirteen "signs" (Libra, Scorpio, Taurus, and so on). The sign you are born under is supposed to affect your character.

THE RITUAL CALENDAR

The second calendar is the tzolk'in, which keeps track of religious events of great significance. This calendar only has thirteen "months" or groups of days, and there are twenty days in each group. This means that the calendar only has 260 days, and a lot of days would happen twice in a year as measured by the solar calendar.

MAYAN CALENDAR STAMPS

Many Mayans, especially in the mountains of Guatemala, still keep the tzolk'in. A special class of "day keepers" maintain the calendar and help the Mayan people know the days for religious observances.

THE CALENDAR ROUND

The Mayan people had a third calendar, the Calendar Round. This combined the jaab and the tzolk'in and tracked individual days over the course of 18,980 days, or 52 years! It would take that long for the same combination from the solar calendar and the ritual calendar to come up again!

Many other cultures in Mexico and Central America also used the Calendar Round.

THE LONG COUNT CALENDAR

The biggest and most impressive calendar of all is the Long Count. This involves five concentric (nested) circles, like gears in a very complex clock. Each day, each circle advances one step, but there are so many combinations that it takes over five thousand years to get to the end of the Long Count!

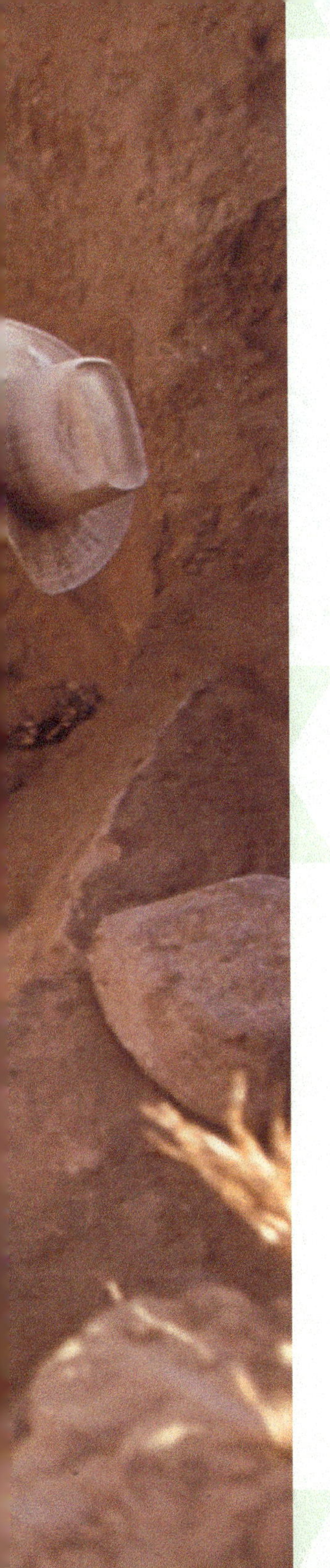

At one level, the Long Count calendar is very useful for historians and archaeologists. If a monument has a Long Count date recorded on it, we can with high confidence figure out what day that was in our calendar. This makes it easier to compare records of kings and great events from different parts of the Mayan Empire.

1 k'in   = 1 day

1 winal   = 20 k'in
             ≈ 3 weeks

1 tun   = 18 winal
             ≈ 1 year

1 k'atun   = 20 tun
             ≈ 20 years

1 b'ak'tun   = 20 k'atun
             ≈ 400 years

When a Long Count date is recorded on a monument, the related date from the Calendar Round is also included.

B'ak'tun 0	starts	11 Aug	3114	BC
B'ak'tun 1	starts	13 Nov	2720	BC
B'ak'tun 2	starts	16 Feb	2325	BC
B'ak'tun 3	starts	21 May	1931	BC
B'ak'tun 4	starts	23 Aug	1537	BC
B'ak'tun 5	starts	26 Nov	1143	BC
B'ak'tun 6	starts	28 Feb	748	BC
B'ak'tun 7	starts	3 Jun	354	BC
B'ak'tun 8	starts	5 Sep	41	
B'ak'tun 9	starts	9 Dec	435	
B'ak'tun 10	starts	13 Mar	830	
B'ak'tun 11	starts	15 Jun	1224	
B'ak'tun 12	starts	18 Sep	1618	
B'ak'tun 13	starts	21 Dec	2012	
B'ak'tun 14	starts	26 Mar	2407	
B'ak'tun 15	starts	28 Jun	2801	
B'ak'tun 16	starts	1 Oct	3195	
B'ak'tun 17	starts	3 Jan	3590	
B'ak'tun 18	starts	7 Apr	3984	
B'ak'tun 19	starts	11 Jul	4378	
Next piktun	starts	13 Oct	4772	

* Dates use the Gregorian calendar

Mesoamerican Long Count calendar

The most recent completion of the Long Count was in December, 2012. In the months leading up to that date, a lot of people became convinced that the world would end on December 11, 2012, at 11:11 in the morning, and that then a fresh, new world would be created. Since you are reading this book, the end of the world must not have happened!

MAYAN WRITING

THE START OF MAYAN WRITING

There was probably an earlier writing system in use in the area where the Mayan culture developed as early as 1000 BCE, but we do not know much about it. It would have been used by the Olmec people, and only a few examples that might be part of this system survived. But the examples we have of this system are very different from what the Mayans created.

The oldest examples of Mayan writing come from inscriptions from around 300 BCE. It is hard to learn much about these early writings, because they have been moved from the place (a tomb or the plaza of a city) where they were first set up. The words, out of context, are very hard to figure out.

MAYAN WRITINGS

WHAT THE LANGUAGE LOOKS LIKE

The Mayans used hieroglyphics, or small images and symbols, to write, rather than letters standing for individual sounds. Mayan writing is very beautiful, but also very complex.

Along with the hieroglyphics used to build up words like the name of a city or a person, or to talk about what happened, there are many other images.

These images are like "emoticons" used in social media today: they aren't part of the words they appear near, but they help you understand those words. There were also symbols to help you understand how to pronounce the word.

MAYA HIEROGLYPHS

A challenge facing modern students of Mayan inscriptions is that there were a lot of dialects of Mayan. It is the same as English-speakers from England and the United States using the same language but having different words for the same things (in England, the storage area in a car is a "boot" while in the United States it is a "trunk").

On top of that, a related tribe, the Yucatec, used the same writing system to make inscriptions in their own language (the way English and French speakers use almost the same set of letters for writing in different languages).

MAYA RUINS, YUCATAN PENINSULA

Making things even harder, when the Spanish armies conquered the Mayan people, they destroyed as much material written in Mayan as

they could. Fortunately, there are thousands of stone inscriptions that were not destroyed.

READING AN INSCRIPTION

Each unit in an inscription is a "glyph". Each glyph can actually be a "sentence" of four or five interlocked glyphs.

An inscription appears in several columns, but you don't read the whole thing left to right, as you are reading this page. Here's how you do it:

Imagine the Mayan inscription has four columns, and each column is a stack of glyphs, so each row has four glyphs (or four sets of nested glyphs). Imagine that the four columns are called A, B, C, and D.

MAYAN HIEROGLYPHS

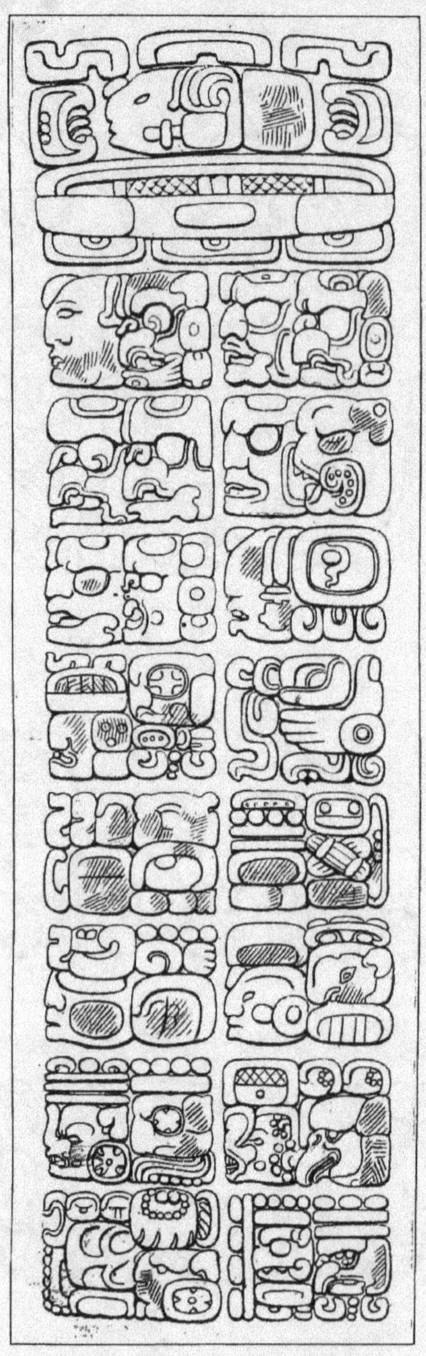

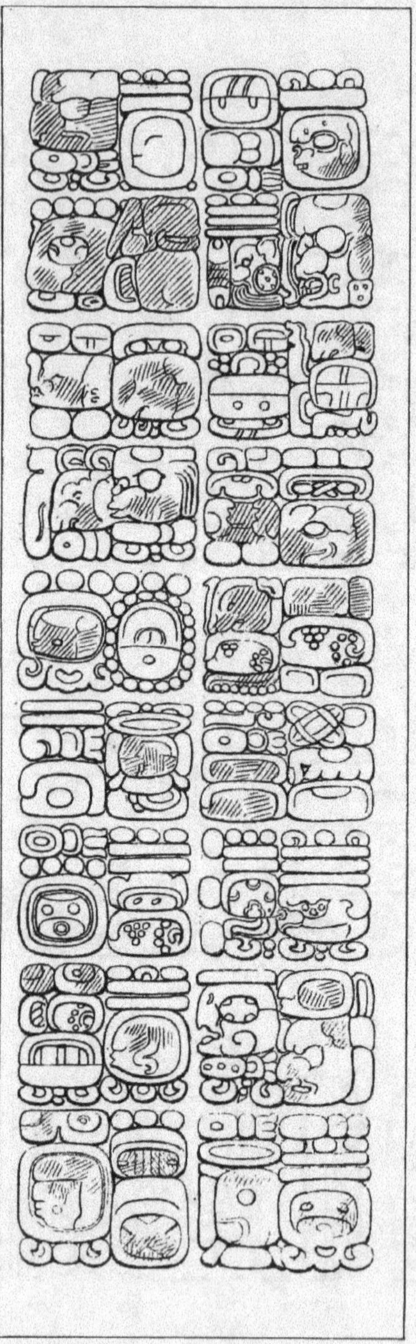

MAYAN HIEROGLYPHS

To read the inscription, you would read the first glyph in column A (A1) and then the first glyph in column B (B1). Then, instead of going on to the other columns, you go down a row and read the next glyph in column A (A2) and the one beside it (B2), and so on. You don't get on to columns C and D until you have reached the bottom of columns A and B.

UNDERSTANDING MAYAN

Those who were trained in writing Mayan could combine glyphs and nested glyphs, plus indicators like emoticons and hints for pronunciation in amazing ways. Trained writers could write the same word in many different ways, probably providing overtones of meaning that we cannot understand now (this is like when you read a text message and might take seriously what was meant as a joke because you can't hear the other person's tone of voice).

a   b   c   d   e

f   g   h   i

j   k   l   m

n   o   p   q

r   s   t   u   v

Modern scholars have spent a long time trying to understand what the stone inscriptions mean, and it took a lot of effort even to figure out what were the names of cities and what were the names of people. Understanding that, and knowing how to read the dates, has made it easier to make educated guesses about what the other words in an inscription might be saying.

LEARN MORE ABOUT THE MAYANS

Although the Mayan Empire was destroyed by the European invasion that started in the 1500s, the Mayan people continued fighting for their independence until 1900. Read about their culture in Baby Professor books like The Mayan Cities, A Quick History of the Mayan Civilization, The Daily Life of a Mayan Family and The Mayans Gave Us their Art and Architecture.

Visit
BABY PROFESSOR
EDUCATION KIDS
www.BabyProfessorBooks.com
to download Free Baby Professor eBooks
and view our catalog of new and exciting
Children's Books